YES! I GOT THE JOB

BENITA BLESSING

AF518142

BlueRose ONE.com
Stories Matter
NewDelhi • London

BLUEROSE PUBLISHERS
India | U.K.

BlueRose ONE.com
Stories Matter
NewDelhi • London

For permissions requests or inquiries regarding this publication, please contact:

BLUEROSE PUBLISHERS
www.BlueRoseONE.com
info@bluerosepublishers.com
+91 8882 898 898
+4407342408967

ISBN: 978-93-6452-012-6

Cover Design: Daksh
Typesetting: Pooja Sharma

First Edition: October 2024

Affirmations

What Are Affirmations?

First, affirmations are phrases or sentences aimed at training the conscious and subconscious mind. They're optimistic, empowering, and focus on positive life outcomes. They might sound a little woo woo, but I encourage you to give them a try!

Why Use Affirmations in Your Job Search?

Your thoughts and beliefs shape your actions and even body language. If you're going into an interview thinking, "I'm not good enough for this job," it's going to affect how you answer the questions and portray yourself in the interview.

I am attracting great opportunities

"I am open to new opportunities and trust that the perfect job for me is on its way." "I am worthy of a great job and I am now attracting it into my life."

I am attracting job opportunities that fit my unique abilities. My career achievements reflect my inner worth and value. I am my own best advocate in my job...

I have all the skills I need to do a great job. ·I grow from every challenge and build onto my knowledge and strengths. · I am a freelancer who my client needs.

Introduction

In a world full of constant changes and evolving career landscapes, I understand the challenges and excitement that come with the journey to find meaningful employment. Whether you're a fresh graduate stepping into the corporate world for the first time or a seasoned professional seeking new opportunities, I've designed this book to be your trusted companion on your path to success. My goal is to offer guidance, insights, and practical advice to help you not only secure a job but also find the right job—one that aligns with your aspirations and empowers you to thrive in your chosen field.

The Search for Meaningful Work

It is not only about seeking the job that pays your bills but also aligns with your passion, interest, and values. It is about securing a position where you can thrive, grow, and make meaningful contributions to your chosen career path.

In the globe where career paths are no longer linear and industries are constantly innovating and modifying, the traditional job-hunting approach is no longer sufficient. It is no longer dust off a cliché resume and send it to a few job postings. Instead, today's job seekers need a unique and comprehensive strategy, a toolkit of skills, and the confidence to navigate the ever-changing job market successfully.

The Importance of Having a Structured Approach

We are surrounded by competitive job markets and diverse career paths and here, a structured approach to job seeking is more important than ever. Gone are the days of simply submitting a resume and hoping for the best. Instead, today's job seekers must be proactive, strategic, and adaptable.

It is not enough to rely on luck or chance when seeking employment. A structured approach provides a clear roadmap, helping you identify your strengths, customize your application materials, target your search efforts, and excel in interviews. It helps you to stand out in a competitive and crowded job market while making you make informed and intellectual decisions.

Your Personal Guide

As you turn the pages of this book and delve into the chapters that follow, you will discover much more than just a collection of tips and techniques for finding a job. This book is your guide, a steadfast companion on your corporate journey toward success.

Consider this book as your knowledgeable mentor, providing you with expert guidance at every turn. It's like having a seasoned career coach by your side, offering insights honed through years of experience.

Job searching can be a lonely journey filled with moments of doubt and uncertainty. That's where this book steps in as your unwavering source of support. It's here to reassure you, answer your questions, and provide solutions to the challenges you might encounter. Whenever you feel overwhelmed or discouraged, remember that you have this book as your constant companion, ready to offer the support and encouragement you need to keep moving forward.

Your Journey Begins Here

Your journey to employment success starts now. It begins with self-discovery, transitions into strategic planning, and culminates in finding a job that fulfills you. Along the way, you'll face challenges, make discoveries, and experience moments of triumph. And through it all, remember that you are not alone. This book is here to help you navigate the path to your dream job.

It is more than just a manual. Each chapter is filled with practical insights, real-world examples, and actionable steps to help you achieve your goals. So, let's dive in and start your journey towards a brighter and more fulfilling future.

Contents

Chapter 1

Self – Assessment

Now let's begin this job-seeking journey not with a search through job listings or an exploration of potential employers, but with a deep and introspective look within ourselves. It is a chapter that takes us on a journey to understand who we are, what we're made of, and where we want to go professionally. It is the starting point of your quest for meaningful employment.

Imagine this chapter as the prologue to a captivating story—a story about your career. It is a story that weaves your unique skills, passions, values, and aspirations into a tapestry of professional fulfillment. But to embark on this journey, you must first understand the characters in this narrative—yourself.

1.1. Know Thyself: Understanding Your Skills and Strengths

Every job seeker has their own set of skills and strengths—unique talents waiting to be uncovered. Think of it as a treasure hunt, where "X" marks the spot, and the treasure is your professional potential. Like a modern-day explorer armed with a magnifying glass, let's begin by examining the landscape of your abilities.

Start by asking yourself: What are you exceptionally good at? What activities or tasks make you feel like you're in your element? Jot down your thoughts, no matter how small or significant they may seem. Are you a skilled communicator, able to express ideas with clarity and conviction? Do you have an innate talent for problem-solving, dissecting complex issues like a detective unraveling a mystery?

To delve even deeper into this treasure trove of talents, consider this: Reach out to your friends, colleagues, or mentors. Sometimes, those closest to us hold a mirror to our abilities, reflecting the qualities that make us shine. Ask them for their honest insights. You might be surprised by the observations they share.

Emily, a recent college graduate, knew the power of self-assessment all too well. Armed with a degree in marketing, she had her sights set on a career that would ignite her passion for creativity and strategy. However, like many job seekers, she faced the daunting question: What makes me stand out in a sea of applicants?

Emily took a seat at her desk, armed with a notebook and determination. As she began to list her skills, she realized that communication was her superpower. She could weave words into compelling stories, captivating the attention of any audience. "Communication skills," she wrote, underlining it twice, a skill that would prove invaluable in her job search.

However, Emily's self-discovery didn't stop there. She knew that her strengths went beyond the ability to craft persuasive messages. She possessed a knack for transforming raw data into actionable insights, a talent that would serve her well in the marketing world. As she pondered this, Emily's list of strengths grew longer and more impressive.

To gain a broader perspective, Emily reached out to her network. She was surprised to hear her colleagues recount stories of her exceptional teamwork during group projects and her ability to infuse life into the dullest of meetings. She was turning mundane discussions into engaging and productive sessions.

Their insights were like gems in her treasure chest of skills and strengths. They were like puzzle pieces, filling in the gaps of her self-awareness. They confirmed her strengths and unveiled hidden talents she hadn't fully appreciated. Emily's journey of self-assessment was not just a solitary endeavor; it was enriched by the perspectives of those who knew her best.

As you embark on your own self-assessment journey, take a page from Emily's book. Don't underestimate the power of your unique skills and strengths. Like her, you might discover talents that set you apart in the job market. Remember that self-discovery is an ongoing process, and insights from those around you can be invaluable in uncovering the full spectrum of your abilities.

1.2. Clarifying Career Goals and Aspirations

Emily's vision was taking shape like a beautiful painting, but she knew that clarity in her career goals was essential to bringing that vision to life. With a growing list of skills, strengths, and a crystal-clear sense of her passions, she was ready to set her career compass.

As Emily visualized her ideal career, she could see herself at the forefront of innovative marketing campaigns. She wanted a role where her creativity would know no bounds, where every day would be an opportunity to craft marketing strategies that not only engaged but inspired people. Her aspirations were not mere whims but a vivid, tangible picture of her future.

"*I want a career that allows me to unleash my creativity,*" she declared with conviction. These words were not just a statement; they were the beginning of her journey to transform her vision into reality.

SMART Goals: The North Star

Emily understood that setting vague, undefined goals would be like navigating without a compass. To ensure she stayed on course, she embraced the **SMART criteria**—Specific, Measurable, Achievable, Relevant, and Time-bound.

- **Specific:** Emily had a precise goal to lead innovative marketing campaigns. This specificity provided a clear target.
- **Measurable:** She wanted to quantify her success, track her progress, and celebrate achievements along the way.
- **Achievable:** Emily's goals were ambitious yet realistic, reflecting her confidence in her abilities.
- **Relevant:** Her aspirations were perfectly aligned with her skills, strengths, and passions, making them meaningful and purposeful.

- **Time-bound:** Emily set deadlines for herself, infusing her goals with a sense of urgency.

This is a valuable reminder of your self-assessment journey. What are your own career aspirations? How does your professional canvas look? Recognize that your goals are more than just distant dreams; they are the navigational stars lighting your way. They provide direction, purpose, and a sense of fulfillment as you embark on your professional path. Whether you're just beginning or seeking a change, setting SMART goals will empower you to turn your aspirations into actionable plans. Remember that your journey, like Emily's, is a work of art waiting to be created; one brushstroke at a time.

1.3. Identifying Personal Values and Interests

While self-assessment often starts with recognizing your skills and setting career goals, it doesn't stop there. It extends into the territory of values and interests, two crucial elements that shape your professional happiness and fulfillment.

Values: The Guiding Principles

Imagine your values as the guiding stars of your life's journey. They are the principles and beliefs that define who you are and what truly matters to you. For Emily, this meant valuing creativity, innovation, and the power to make a difference. These values were not confined to her work life alone; they permeated every aspect of her existence.

In the quest for meaningful employment, understanding your values is like having a compass. It helps you navigate towards opportunities that align with your principles. If, like Emily, you value creativity, you'll thrive in a role that encourages and celebrates innovation.

Consider this quote by Maya Angelou: "*Success is liking yourself, liking what you do, and liking how you do it.*" It reinforces the idea that aligning your values with your work is a significant component of success.

Interests: The Clues to Your Passions

While values guide your overarching principles, interests delve into the specifics of what excites and fulfills you. Emily's journey wasn't confined to the office; she sought fulfillment outside of work through writing, painting, and volunteering. These were more than hobbies; they were the sparks that ignited her passion.

Your interests are like breadcrumbs leading you toward a career that resonates with your heart. They reveal your true passions. For Emily, writing wasn't just a pastime; it was a glimpse into her love for storytelling and communication. Her passion for painting uncovered her artistic side, and volunteering allowed her to make a meaningful impact on her community.

Consider this wisdom from Albert Schweitzer: "*Success is not the key to happiness. Happiness is the key to success. If you love what you are doing, you will be successful.*" It underscores the importance of pursuing work that aligns with your interests and passions. When your job resonates with your heart, it's not just work; it's a source of joy and fulfillment.

As you embark on your own self-assessment journey, take time to reflect on your values and interests. What principles guide your life? What activities make your heart sing? Understanding these aspects of yourself will not only help you find a job but also a career that aligns with your true self. Your journey of self-discovery is a powerful tool in your quest for meaningful employment, one that leads to professional fulfillment and personal satisfaction. Remember, the road ahead is filled with promise and possibilities, guided by the stars of your values and the sparks of your interests.

Self-assessment is a foundational building block for your entire career. You've delved into the depths of your skills, strengths, values, aspirations, and interests, uncovering the unique tapestry that makes you who you are.

Just as Emily discovered the power of self-awareness and the treasures hidden within herself, you too have the potential to unearth your own riches. The skills and strengths you possess, the goals and dreams you hold dear, the values that guide your moral compass, and the passions that fuel your spirit—all of these elements will shape your path to meaningful employment.

As you turn the page to the next chapter, remember that your story is unfolding, and you are the author of your own narrative. Your quest for meaningful employment has only just begun, and the adventure ahead is brimming with promise and possibilities. Stay curious, stay determined, and keep moving forward, for your professional destiny awaits.

Chapter 2

Build a Strong Foundation

In the previous chapter, we embarked on the quest of self-assessment, a crucial first step in your job-seeking adventure. Now, in this chapter, we'll delve into the nuts and bolts of building a strong foundation for your job-seeking journey. It's time to roll up your sleeves and get to work on crafting the essential tools that will make you stand out in the competitive job market.

As we discussed, understanding your skills, strengths, values, aspirations, and interests is like laying the groundwork for a grand adventure. However, drawing from my years of experience as a recruiter, I can attest that having the right tools is essential to navigate this journey effectively. This chapter is all about equipping you with those essential tools. So, let's dive right in.

2.1. How to Craft a Strong Resume: Your Path to Standing Out

Picture this: you're in a room filled with other job seekers, all vying for the same opportunity. Your resume is your ticket to stand out in the crowd, your first impression of a potential employer. It needs to be more than just a list of past jobs; it should be a captivating story of your professional journey.

Let me introduce you to Alex, a determined young professional with a solid background in marketing.

Despite his credentials, he faced a common struggle—his initial resume was drowning in a sea of mundane job descriptions. But with a bit of guidance and a sprinkle of creativity, he transformed his resume into a powerful narrative of his accomplishments.

One particular achievement stood out: Alex had orchestrated a remarkable 50% increase in a client's social media engagement in just three months. When he added this accomplishment to his revamped resume, the response was astounding. Not only did he start receiving interview invitations, but he also clinched a job offer from a prestigious marketing agency.

Now let's dive into the art of crafting a resume that leaves a lasting impact:

Clarity is Key

Imagine a busy recruiter, sifting through a mountain of resumes. They don't have the time to decipher a cluttered document. Your resume should be a beacon of clarity. Use well-defined headings, concise bullet points, and a consistent format. Make it effortless for recruiters to find the information they need.

Organization

A clean format helps you organize your resume logically. You can use sections like "Summary," "Work Experience," "Skills," and "Education" to categorize your information. This structure guides the reader through your resume, making it a cohesive and coherent document.

Readability

Avoid using overly complex layouts, fonts, or colors. Stick to a professional and easy-to-read design. A clean format ensures that your resume is visually appealing and can be easily viewed on various devices and platforms.

Highlight Your Achievements

A common mistake is merely listing job responsibilities. Instead, focus on your accomplishments. Paint a vivid picture of how you made a difference in your previous roles. Use quantifiable metrics to show the impact you've had. For instance, rather than stating you "managed a marketing campaign," proudly declare that you "skyrocketed website traffic by 30% through a brilliantly executed marketing campaign."

Tailor for the Job

One-size-fits-all doesn't work in the world of resumes. Customizing your resume for each job application is like tailoring a suit for a special occasion—it's a mark of dedication and genuine interest in the role. Let me explain why this step is so crucial from my perspective as a recruiter.

When I review a resume that has been tailored to match the specific job requirements, it stands out immediately. It tells me that the candidate has done their homework, understands the nuances of the position, and is genuinely invested in the opportunity. It's like a candidate saying, "I'm not just looking for any job; I want *this* job."

Here's why customization matters:

- **It Aligns with the Job Description**

Every job posting is unique, with its own set of qualifications and requirements. Tailoring your resume ensures that you showcase the skills and experiences most relevant to that particular job. It's like fitting puzzle pieces together; the more they match, the clearer the picture becomes.

- **It Highlights Your Fit**

Customization demonstrates that you are the right fit for the role. It's not just about listing your skills; it's about connecting the dots between your background and what the employer is looking for. It's a way of saying, "I've got what it takes, and here's the proof."

- **It Saves the Recruiter's Time**

Recruiters often have limited time to review each resume. When your resume is customized, it's easier for us to see that you meet the key criteria. It's like giving us a roadmap. We can quickly navigate your qualifications and decide if you're a strong candidate.

- **It Sets You Apart**

In a sea of generic resumes, a tailored one is a breath of fresh air. It shows that you're willing to put in the effort, and it makes you memorable. When I discuss candidates with my team, those who've tailored their resumes stand out in our conversations.

Don't Include Irrelevant Information

Recruiters are looking for specific qualifications and experiences that match the job they're hiring for. When you include irrelevant information, you dilute the impact of your resume. It's like telling a story with an unnecessary plot twist, it distracts from the main narrative.

Including irrelevant information can give the impression that you don't understand the requirements of the job or that you're trying to compensate for a lack of relevant experience. It's like trying to fit a square peg into a round hole, it just doesn't work.

Maintain Truthfulness

One of the cardinal rules of resume writing is to always be truthful. Exaggerating your achievements or qualifications may seem tempting, but it's a risky strategy that can backfire in multiple ways. First and foremost, honesty is key to building trust and credibility with potential employers. It's like starting a relationship with a lie, it undermines the foundation of trust.

Many employers conduct reference checks before making a job offer. If your previous employers or references provide information that contradicts what's on your resume, it can lead to a lost job opportunity and damage your professional reputation.

So, from my perspective as a recruiter, I can't stress enough how important it is to customize your resume. It's a powerful way to demonstrate your commitment and increase your chances of landing the job you truly want.

The lesson here is crystal clear—your resume isn't just a document; it's your opportunity to shine. Your achievements are the stars of this show, and with the right spotlight, they can make all the difference in your job search.

2.2. How to Write a Compelling Cover Letter

Just as a well-crafted map complements a treasure hunter's tools, your cover letter complements your resume. It's your chance to share your story, motivations, and why you're the perfect fit for the job.

Meet Michael, a college graduate with a degree in environmental science. He was passionate about sustainability and dreamt of working for a renowned environmental organization. One day, he came across a job posting for an entry-level environmental researcher position at his dream organization.

The Opening Act

In his cover letter, Michael began by recalling a personal experience from his childhood. He described how, as a young boy, he would spend weekends volunteering at a local nature conservation group with his family. He vividly recounted his excitement at planting trees, cleaning up parks, and learning about the importance of protecting the environment.

Body Language Matters

Michael's cover letter went on to explain how this early exposure to environmental conservation had shaped his career aspirations. He shared his academic achievements and relevant coursework, emphasizing his dedication to environmental research.

Radiate Enthusiasm

What made Michael's cover letter stand out was his evident enthusiasm for the organization. He expressed his admiration for the organization's groundbreaking research and conservation efforts. Michael's letter wasn't just about why he was a good fit for the role; it was also about why the organization was a perfect fit for his passion and values.

A Tale of Tailoring

Michael didn't stop there. He carefully tailored his cover letter to the specific role. He discussed the organization's recent research projects and publications, mentioning how inspired he was by their work. He even cited a recent study published by the organization and shared his thoughts on it.

The Power of Storytelling

Michael's story didn't go unnoticed. The hiring manager was captivated by his cover letter and saw in him, not just a qualified candidate but someone genuinely passionate about their cause. Michael was not only invited for an interview but was also offered the position.

His cover letter had made a significant impact. It demonstrated that Michael wasn't just looking for any job; he was seeking an opportunity to contribute to a cause he deeply cared about. The organization recognized the potential in his passion and skills, making Michael's dream of working in environmental research a reality.

This real-life example illustrates how a compelling cover letter can transform a job application from a mere submission to a powerful narrative that resonates with employers. It's a testament to the idea that your cover letter isn't just a formality; it's a chance to tell your story and connect with your potential employer on a personal level.

2.3. How to Create a Strong Profile on LinkedIn and Other Platforms

In the digital age, your online presence is as important as your physical resume. Platforms like LinkedIn, GitHub, or personal websites can be your allies in the job-seeking journey. They offer an extended version of your resume, complete with interactive features that let you showcase your expertise.

LinkedIn: Your Professional Showcase

LinkedIn is the go-to platform for professionals, and having a standout profile here is non-negotiable. It's not just an online resume; it's your digital professional identity. Here's how to make it shine:

- **Profile Photo**

Use a high-quality, professional-looking photo where you're dressed appropriately for your industry. A friendly and approachable expression goes a long way.

- **Compelling Headline**

Your headline should be more than just your job title. Craft a concise yet impactful headline that conveys your value and expertise. For example, instead of "Marketing

Manager," you could say "Digital Marketing Strategist | SEO Expert | Content Creator."

- **Summary Statement**

Your LinkedIn summary is your opportunity to tell your professional story. It should be engaging and informative, providing a snapshot of your background, skills, and career goals. Use this space to highlight what sets you apart.

- **Work Experience**

Just like your resume, your LinkedIn work experience should emphasize your achievements and contributions. Use bullet points to showcase your accomplishments in each role.

- **Skills and Endorsements**

List relevant skills on your profile, and don't be shy about asking colleagues and connections to endorse you for them. A well-endorsed skill set adds credibility.

- **Recommendations**

Request recommendations from supervisors, colleagues, or clients who can vouch for your work. These third-party endorsements carry weight.

- **Engagement**

Actively engage with your network. Share insightful articles, comment on posts, and participate in discussions related to your field. This showcases your industry knowledge.

Other Platforms: Tailoring to Your Industry

LinkedIn might be the primary platform for professionals, but depending on your field, other platforms can be equally important. For instance, if you're in the creative industry, having a robust portfolio on platforms like Behance or Dribble can be invaluable. If you're in tech, a strong GitHub profile might be essential. Tailor your online presence to align with the expectations of your industry.

Content is King

Lastly, consider creating and sharing content relevant to your field. Write articles, create videos, or curate content that demonstrates your expertise. Consistent and valuable content can position you as a thought leader in your industry.

In this digital age, your online presence can be just as influential as your in-person interactions. By crafting a compelling LinkedIn profile and tailoring your presence to your industry's expectations, you'll be well on your way to making a lasting impression on potential employers.

2.4. How to Develop a Strong Online Presence

In today's interconnected world, a strong online presence is essential for job seekers. Chapter 2 wouldn't be complete without a section on developing a robust online presence. Let's dive into how you can establish a strong presence on the internet.

Leverage Social Media

Use platforms like Twitter, Facebook, and even Instagram to your advantage. Follow companies you're interested in, engage with industry leaders, and share insightful content. Just remember to keep your personal profiles professional.

Personal Website or Blog

If you have the time and inclination, consider creating a personal website or blog. This is an excellent way to showcase your expertise, share your thoughts on industry trends, and provide a portfolio of your work.

Online Portfolios

If you're in a creative field like design, writing, or photography, having an online portfolio is a must. Websites like Behance, Medium, or even a dedicated portfolio website can help you display your work.

Professional Networking

Join professional networking sites and forums related to your industry. Actively participate in discussions, ask questions, and contribute your insights. This not only establishes your presence but also helps you stay updated on industry news.

Online Courses and Certifications

Enroll in online courses or earn certifications relevant to your field. This not only enhances your skills but also demonstrates your commitment to continuous learning.

Google Yourself

Regularly search for your name on Google to see what comes up. Make sure your online presence is professional and that there's nothing that could harm your reputation.

Privacy Settings

Adjust the privacy settings on your personal social media accounts to ensure they're not visible to potential employers. You want them to see your professional side, not your vacation photos.

By following these guidelines and ensuring your online presence is professional, you'll be well on your way to impressing potential employers and establishing yourself as a serious contender in your field. Remember, in today's digital age, your online presence can be a powerful asset in your job-seeking journey.

As we wrap up this chapter, I want to leave you with this thought: Building a strong foundation for your job-seeking adventure is like constructing a solid bridge to your dream career. As a recruiter, I've seen these tools in action, transforming ordinary job applications into compelling narratives that resonate with hiring managers. And I've seen how a strong online presence can position you as a serious contender in your field. Now you're ready to embark on the next phase of your journey.

Chapter 3

Job Searching Strategies and Networking

Hello again, fellow job seekers! Welcome to the next chapter of our adventure in the world of meaningful employment. In this chapter, we're going to dive deep into the world of job-searching strategies and networking. Now, why is this important, you ask? Well, let me tell you, it's like having a treasure map in your quest for that dream job.

You see, job hunting is a bit like a grand adventure. You're the brave explorer, and the job market is your uncharted territory. But you don't want to go in blind and that's where job-searching strategies come into play. They're like the map that guides you through the dense jungle of job listings, helping you discover hidden opportunities.

And what's a great adventure without companions? That's where networking comes in. Think of it as assembling a crew of allies who can help you on your journey. Together, you'll navigate treacherous waters and uncover the most coveted treasures that are job opportunities tailored to your aspirations.

So, let's set sail, fellow job seekers, as we explore the strategies and networking tactics that will make your job hunt a legendary quest.

3.1. The Job–Seekers Treasure Map: Navigating Job Searching Platforms

Imagine you're a sailor embarking on a treasure hunt. To find the hidden riches, you need a reliable map and the right tools. In the world of job-seeking, job searching platforms serve as your treasure map. They are the compasses that help you navigate the vast sea of job opportunities. This section is all about understanding these platforms and how to use them effectively.

General Job Boards

Think of these as the bustling marketplaces of job listings. As we've previously explored in the previous chapter, websites such as LinkedIn, Indeed, and Glassdoor serve as expansive fishing grounds where you can cast your net wide to uncover a diverse array of job openings. They are like the central hubs of job postings, covering a wide range of industries and positions. Whether you're a recent graduate or a seasoned professional, you'll find a plethora of opportunities here. It's like a bustling bazaar where you can explore jobs from various sectors all in one place.

Industry-Specific Websites

Sometimes, you're on a quest for something more specialized. These are the specialized platforms tailored to certain professions or fields. While we touched upon these websites briefly in the previous chapter, here we'll delve into them more extensively, offering you comprehensive guidance on harnessing their full potential for your job search. For example, GitHub Jobs is a paradise for techies. If you're a software developer, designer, or tech enthusiast, you're likely to find your dream job here. Similarly, Behance and Dribble are havens for creative minds, offering a treasure trove of opportunities in the art and design world. It's like entering a hidden cave filled with treasures specific to your expertise.

Company Websites

Ah, the treasures hidden in plain sight! Many companies prefer to post job openings on their own websites before anywhere else. This means if there's a specific company you're interested in working for, visiting their official website should be a top priority. You might just stumble upon the hidden gems first. It's like searching for buried treasure right in the company's backyard, where only the most dedicated explorers will find them.

In the next sections, we'll delve deeper into how to make the most of these platforms, explore various job searching methods, and uncover industry-specific job opportunities. Think of it as equipping yourself with the finest tools and strategies for your job-seeking adventure. So, grab your compass, and let's navigate this treasure map together!

3.2. Exploring Job Searching Methods: Beyond the CV Drops

In this section, we'll explore smart approaches that can make your job hunt more focused. There's more to success than just dropping your CV like confetti and hoping for the best. We have to delve into strategic job searching methods that go beyond the usual routine. Think of these methods as your treasure map, guiding you to opportunities you might not have otherwise discovered.

From the power of networking to the art of cold outreach and the invaluable assistance of recruitment agencies, we're about to uncover valuable insights that will elevate your job search game.

Networking: Your Ultimate Treasure Map

Networking is not just about collecting connections on LinkedIn and forgetting about them. It is about building genuine relationships with professionals in your field. These connections can be your ticket to opportunities you didn't even know existed. So, don't be a passive observer; engage, contribute, and be an active part of professional communities. The person you chat with today could be the one introducing you to your dream job tomorrow.

Cold Outreach: Blaze Your Trail

Ever heard the phrase, "Fortune favors the bold"? Well, it applies to job searching too. Sometimes, the most exciting opportunities are hidden in plain sight. Don't hesitate to reach out to companies you admire, even if they aren't actively advertising job openings. This proactive approach shows your genuine interest and can lead to creating opportunities that weren't there before. It's like being an explorer in a new land, forging a path where others haven't ventured yet.

Recruitment Agencies: Your Job-Seeking Guides

Think of recruitment agencies as your trusted guides in the wild terrain of job seeking. These agencies specialize in matching candidates with the right opportunities. They have insider knowledge about job openings that might not be publicly advertised. By partnering with a reputable recruitment agency, you gain access to a network of employers actively seeking talent. It's like having a personal scout who knows where the hidden treasures (jobs) are buried.

3.3. Pirate Parties and Job-Shopping Sprees: Networking Events and Job Fairs

It's time to don your networking eyepatch and embark on some pirate-style adventures at networking events and job fairs. These events are your treasure troves of opportunities. Here's what you need to know:

Networking Events

Think of networking events as gatherings of like-minded job-adventurers, all seeking new opportunities on the job-seeking seas. These events come in various forms, from industry conferences to meetups hosted by professional organizations. At networking events, you have the chance to chat, mingle, and, if you're skilled, leave with valuable contacts and potential job opportunities.

For example, imagine you're a software developer looking to advance your career. Attending a tech conference allows you to connect with fellow developers, industry experts, and even representatives from tech companies. By striking up conversations, sharing your experiences, and showing genuine interest in others, you can build a network of contacts who might later refer you to job openings or invite you to apply at their companies.

Job Fairs

Job fairs are like shopping malls for job seekers. Picture a bustling marketplace where multiple companies set up shop under one roof, eagerly handing out job opportunities like prized treasures. These events offer a fantastic chance to explore various job options, gather information about different companies, and make a lasting impression on potential employers.

Let's suppose you're a recent college graduate eager to kick-start your career in marketing. Attending a job fair featuring companies from diverse industries gives you a unique opportunity to interact directly with recruiters. You can learn about their company cultures, job openings, and application processes. Make sure your "shopping cart" (your resume) is ready to be filled with brochures, business cards, and, if all goes well, potential job offers.

Remember that every step in this adventure brings you closer to your goal. With the right strategies, networks, and a sense of adventure, you'll navigate the job-seeking seas with confidence. I want to emphasize that your job-seeking journey is an exciting adventure. By equipping yourself with the right tools and strategies, you're taking the helm of your career destiny.

Chapter 4

The Application Process

It's time to embark on the fourth leg of our journey towards securing that dream job. In this chapter, we're delving deep into the application process. Now, you might be thinking, "Applying for a job? I've got that covered." But trust me, there's more to this than meets the eye. We're about to step on a journey that will equip you with the knowledge and skills needed to conquer the application process. From the intricacies of submitting online applications to deciphering assessments and tests, and finally, the fine art of follow-up, we've got it all covered. So, fasten your seatbelts, and let's unravel the mysteries of successful job applications.

4.1. The Art of Applying: A Complete Guide

Welcome to the heart of the application process, where we'll equip you with the knowledge and skills needed to embark on your job-seeking adventure. Think of this as your treasure map to mastering the art of applying for a job.

Your Application Kit

Just as a seasoned sailor equips themselves with the right gear, you need a well-organized application kit. We'll explore the essential components, including your trusty resume, a captivating cover letter, and any additional documents requested by the employer. Your application kit is your toolkit, and each piece plays a vital role in your quest for the perfect job.

Customizing Your Application

Each job application is like a unique treasure chest waiting to be unlocked, but there's no one-size-fits-all key. Discover the art of customization and learn how to tailor your application to match the specific job requirements as we thoroughly discussed in the second chapter. Just as a skilled navigator adjusts their course to the seas, you'll adapt your application to the job's specific needs.

The Online Application

Navigating online applications can feel like charting your course through digital waters. We'll be your virtual compass, guiding you through the ins and outs of online applications. Understand why they're essential in today's job market and discover the key elements you need to prepare. From uploading your resume to answering application questions, we'll ensure you're well-prepared for this part of your journey.

In the following sections, we'll delve deeper into these aspects, providing you with practical advice and real-world examples. By the time we're done, you'll be well-prepared to tackle any job application with confidence, as if you were embarking on a well-orchestrated sailing adventure. So, hoist the sails, and let's set sail into the world of job applications!

4.2. Submitting Online Applications: How and Why

Welcome to the digital frontier of job applications! In this section, we'll unveil the importance of online applications and provide you with the knowledge and strategies needed to conquer this aspect of your job-seeking adventure.

The Digital Frontier

First, let's set sail by exploring why online applications have become the preferred method for employers. In this digital age, online applications are the bridges connecting job seekers to potential employers. They have become the primary means through which job seekers interact with companies. However, successfully navigating the digital waters of job applications requires a set of essential skills and strategies.

Creating a Winning Online Profile

Your online profile is your ship's appearance on the open digital seas. We'll guide you on how to build a remarkable digital presence, particularly on platforms like LinkedIn. Your online profile serves as your digital resume and can significantly enhance your job applications. We'll explore how to showcase your skills, accomplishments, and expertise to make a lasting impression on potential employers. Think of it as adorning your ship with eye-catching sails that draw attention.

Your online profile essentially serves as your digital resume, and making it stand out can significantly enhance your job applications. Some of the essential steps are mentioned below:

1. **Read Job Descriptions Carefully:** Before applying, thoroughly read the job description to understand the role's requirements and responsibilities.
2. **Tailor Your Resume:** Customize your resume for each application. Highlight the skills and experiences that align with the specific job you're applying for.
3. **Cover Letter:** Craft a compelling cover letter that addresses the hiring manager directly, briefly summarizes your qualifications, and explains why you're an ideal candidate for the position.
4. **Application Tracking System (ATS):** Be aware that many employers use ATS software to screen resumes. Use relevant keywords from the job description to increase your chances of passing through this initial screening.
5. **Attachments:** Ensure that all required documents, such as resumes, cover letters, and certifications, are correctly attached in the preferred format (usually PDF).
6. **Professional Email Address:** Use a professional email address when applying, ideally one that includes your name, to make a positive impression.
7. **Confirmation:** After submitting your application, confirm receipt with a follow-up email. Express your continued interest in the position and inquire about the expected timeline for responses.

By following these practical steps, you'll not only enhance your online presence but also streamline your online application process. I have already explained some of the points thoroughly in previous chapters. However, these actions are particularly important to implement during the application process. It will increase your chances of making a memorable impression on potential employers and successfully navigating the digital waters of job applications.

4.3. Navigating Assessments and Tests

In the modern world of recruitment, employers have raised their flags and introduced a variety of assessments and tests to evaluate potential crew members. While it might feel like navigating through unknown waters, worry not; we've got your back on how to tackle these challenges.

Understanding Assessment Types

Just as different ships are built for different purposes, assessments and tests come in various forms. You may encounter skills assessments that evaluate your technical expertise, cognitive assessments testing your problem-solving skills, or even personality assessments gauging your fit with the company culture. In this section, we'll help you decipher the specific assessment types and what to expect from each.

Preparing for Assessments

Preparation is like the sturdy hull of your ship, keeping you afloat during the roughest of assessments. We'll provide you with essential strategies to get ready for these evaluations. Whether it's brushing up on your technical knowledge, practicing problem-solving scenarios, or gaining insights into personality tests, you'll be well-prepared to sail through them.

Handling Online Interviews

In today's digital age, interviews often take place in the virtual realm. This includes video interviews and assessments, which can be quite different from traditional in-person meetings. We'll guide you on how to prepare for these online interactions and how to excel in them. From setting up your ideal interview space to mastering video interview etiquette, we've got you covered.

Here's a brief guide on how to handle them:

1. **Prepare Your Environment:** Find a quiet, well-lit space for your interview. Ensure your background is tidy and free from distractions.
2. **Test Your Equipment:** Before the interview, make sure your camera, microphone, and internet connection are all working correctly. Conduct a test call to a friend or family member to check audio and video quality.
3. **Dress Professionally:** Dress as you would for an in-person interview. This not only shows respect for the process but also helps you feel more confident.
4. **Body Language Matters:** Maintain eye contact by looking at your webcam, not the screen. Sit up straight and avoid excessive fidgeting.
5. **Practice:** If you're doing a recorded interview with preset questions, practice your responses beforehand. Keep your answers concise and focused.

6. **Technology Backup:** Have a backup plan ready in case of technical difficulties. This might include having a phone number to call in case of a video conferencing failure.

7. **Be Yourself:** Don't forget to be yourself. Online interviews can feel impersonal, but remember to convey your enthusiasm for the position and the company.

8. **Follow-Up:** After the interview, send a thank-you email, just as you would for an in-person interview. Express your appreciation for the opportunity and your continued interest in the role.

4.4. The Art of Follow-Up: Navigating the Waters After You Apply

Your adventure doesn't end with submitting your application. Following up is a crucial part of the process. Let's explore why follow-up is important and how you can do it effectively.

Why Follow-Up After Application Is Important

Imagine this: your application is a message in a bottle, cast into the sea of job applications. Without follow-up, it might drift unnoticed or be lost among countless others. Here's why follow-up is essential:

- **Demonstrates Enthusiasm:**

Following up shows your genuine interest in the position. Employers appreciate candidates who are enthusiastic about joining their team.

- **Keeps You Top-of-Mind:**

In the competitive job market, employers review numerous applications. A well-timed follow-up can remind them of your candidacy.

- **Addresses Concerns:**

Sometimes, employers may have questions or concerns about your application. A follow-up allows you to clarify any uncertainties.

- **Strengthens Your Personal Brand:**

A professional and polite follow-up reinforces your positive image, demonstrating your communication skills and professionalism.

How to Follow Up After Application

Now, let's dive into how you can navigate the art of follow-up:

1. **Wait for a Response:** Give the employer a reasonable amount of time to review applications before following up. Typically, a week is a good benchmark.
2. **Craft a Polite Email:** Compose a concise and polite follow-up email. Express your continued interest in the position and inquire about the application's status.
3. **Subject Line Matters:** Use a clear and professional subject line, such as "Follow-Up on [Position Name] Application."

4. **Highlight Your Qualifications:** In your email, briefly reiterate your relevant qualifications and enthusiasm for the role.

5. **Ask About Next Steps:** Politely inquire about the timeline for the hiring process and any upcoming steps.

6. **Avoid Being Overbearing:** One follow-up email is usually sufficient. Repeated, frequent follow-ups can be perceived as pushy.

7. **Thank You:** Express your gratitude for the opportunity to apply and thank the employer for their time.

By understanding the art of applying, why online applications are essential, creating an impressive online profile, and mastering the follow-up, you're not just a job seeker; you're a seasoned explorer. Your approach is deliberate, your skills honed, and your enthusiasm unwavering.

Now, as we venture into the next chapter, we'll delve into the heart of the hiring process - interviews. Get ready to sharpen your conversational cutlass, for we'll uncover strategies, techniques, and tips to ensure you shine during these crucial conversations.

Chapter 5

Preparation for Interview

The voyage to securing your dream job continues, and in this chapter, we'll be your navigators as we sail into the waters of interview preparation. By now, you've mastered the art of job application, and the treasure map of your qualifications has brought you to the shores of opportunity. The next challenge? The interview, where you'll meet your potential employers.

As seasoned sailors of the job-seeking seas know, "First impressions are lasting." An interview is your opportunity to create a memorable impression and demonstrate your worth to the company. This chapter is designed to be your compass in these uncharted waters, guiding you through the intricacies of interview preparation.

5.1. Crafting Your Interview Game Plan

Much like a shrewd strategist plotting their moves, you need a clear game plan for your upcoming interview. Here's your guide to creating a roadmap:

Understanding the Company and Role

Before stepping into the interview, make sure you have a solid grasp of the company's background, culture, and the specifics of the role you're vying for. This knowledge won't just display your genuine interest but also arm you with insightful information.

Picture yourself interviewing for a marketing position with a company renowned for its cutting-edge digital campaigns. Mentioning your familiarity with their recent award-winning project showcases your enthusiasm and research skills.

Company Research

Delve into the company's history, values, and noteworthy achievements. For instance, if you're interviewing at a tech startup recognized for its inventive solutions, your knowledge of their recent groundbreaking work reflects your genuine interest.

For example, in an interview with a company celebrated for revolutionizing renewable energy solutions, discussing their recent breakthroughs and your eagerness to contribute your expertise in sustainability demonstrates your commitment.

Role Familiarity:

Analyze the job description meticulously. Understand the key responsibilities, desired skills, and qualifications. Establish connections between these requirements and your own experiences and be prepared with relevant examples.

Let's say you're interviewing for a Data Analyst role. The job description places a strong emphasis on data visualization skills. You can narrate an incident from your prior job where your adept data visualization improved decision-making processes and drove significant results, aligning with their criteria.

By following these strategies, you'll be superbly prepared for your interview. You'll not only make a strong impression but also underscore your authentic interest in the company and your aptitude for the role.

5.2. Mastering Common Questions

Interviews frequently include a set of standard questions that you should be well-prepared to tackle. We're here to provide expert guidance and concrete examples of how to craft your responses to some of these commonly asked questions:

1. Tell me about yourself:

This open-ended question is your opportunity to give a concise overview of your professional journey. Focus on your most relevant experiences and achievements. Keep it professional and avoid personal details.

"I'm a marketing professional with over five years of experience. I've worked in various industries, developing and implementing successful digital marketing campaigns. My expertise lies in data analysis, which allows me to make data-driven decisions for optimizing campaigns and delivering tangible results."

2. Why do you want to work here:

Show your interviewer that you've done your homework and are genuinely interested in the company. Discuss how your skills align with their values and mission.

"I want to work at XYZ Company because of its reputation for innovation and commitment to sustainability, which aligns with my values. Your recent project on [mention a project] particularly impressed me. I believe my expertise in [your expertise] can contribute to such groundbreaking initiatives."

3. What are your strengths and weaknesses:

Highlight your strengths, focusing on those relevant to the job. When addressing weaknesses, be honest but frame them as areas for improvement and show how you're working on them.

(Strengths): "One of my key strengths is my ability to adapt to new technologies quickly. In my previous role at XYZ Company, I learned and became proficient in a new analytics tool within weeks, streamlining our data analysis process."

(Weaknesses): "I tend to be overly critical of my work, which can sometimes slow me down. However, I've been actively working on striking a balance between striving for perfection and meeting deadlines."

4. Why should we hire you:

This question is your chance to sell yourself. Highlight your unique skills and experiences and explain how they'll benefit the company.

"You should hire me because I bring a combination of experience in [mention your skills], a track record of success at [mention relevant accomplishments], and a strong commitment to [Company's mission/values]. I'm confident that I can contribute to [specific project or goal] and help [Company] continue its growth and success."

5. Where do you see yourself in five years:

This question assesses your long-term career goals and your alignment with the company's opportunities for growth.

"In five years, I see myself in a leadership role within the company, potentially in a position where I can contribute to strategy and mentor team members. I'm committed to continuously learning and growing, and I believe [Company] provides the perfect environment for achieving those goals."

These examples provide a framework for crafting your own responses to common interview questions. Tailor them to your experiences and the specific job you're interviewing for.

5.3. Practice Makes Perfect: Why and How

Just as an accomplished craftsman practices their trade before undertaking a significant project, you must never enter an interview unprepared. Find out why practice is crucial and learn how to effectively execute it:

Mock Interviews:

Consider conducting mock interviews, whether with a friend or by utilizing technology. These simulated interviews will serve to build your confidence and refine your responses. Practice addressing common interview questions and situational inquiries. Additionally, receive constructive feedback to help identify areas for improvement.

Speaking Clearly:

Practicing your responses and articulating them clearly and succinctly is vital. Avoid unnecessary rambling, which can lead to a loss of focus. Utilize practice sessions to refine your answers, ensuring they are well-structured and to the point.

By engaging in mock interviews and focusing on articulating your responses clearly, you'll be better prepared to confidently navigate the actual interview. These practices will enhance your performance and increase your chances of leaving a positive impression on the interviewers.

5.4. Navigating Body Language and Outer Appearance

Just as a seasoned actor uses body language and attire to convey a character's personality, you must leverage these tools to make a positive impression during your interview. We'll guide you on projecting confidence through your body language and outer appearance:

Dress for Success

Understanding the appropriate attire is crucial. Whether you're heading into a corporate setting, a creative environment, or somewhere in between, knowing what to wear can significantly impact the interviewer's perception of you. Here are the dos and don'ts of interview outfits:

Dos:

1. **Research the Company Culture:** Investigate the company's dress code and culture to align your attire with their expectations. A more traditional corporation might require a suit, while a startup might prefer business casual or even something more casual.
2. **Choose Neutral Colors:** Opt for neutral colors like black, navy, gray, and white. These are safe choices that convey professionalism.
3. **Ensure Proper Fit:** Ill-fitting clothes can be distracting and give off an unprofessional impression. Make sure your attire is well-fitted and tailored to your body.
4. **Pay Attention to Grooming:** Neat and well-groomed hair, clean nails, and an overall polished appearance are essential. Your appearance should reflect your attention to detail.
5. **Wear Comfortable Shoes:** Comfort is key. You might be on your feet or walking around the office. Choose shoes that are both professional and comfortable.

Don'ts:

1. **Avoid Flashy Accessories:** It's best to keep accessories like jewelry and ties understated. Flashy accessories can be distracting.
2. **Say No to Strong Fragrances:** Overwhelming fragrances can be unpleasant to interviewers. Opt for a light, subtle fragrance if you choose to wear one.

3. **Don't Experiment with New Clothes:** The day of the interview is not the time to wear brand-new clothes. Make sure your outfit is tried and tested for comfort and suitability.
4. **Stay Away from Revealing or Casual Attire:** Avoid low-cut tops, short skirts, or overly casual attire. Dress modestly and professionally.
5. **Limit Bright Colors:** While bright colors can be eye-catching, it's best to stick with neutrals during interviews. They are less likely to be distracting.

Maintaining Eye Contact

Eye contact is a fundamental element of non-verbal communication. It's the equivalent of your ship's steady course on the open seas, indicating your confidence and interest. We'll guide you on the importance of maintaining eye contact during the interview, helping you connect with the interviewers, and conveying your enthusiasm for the position.

Now, as you embark on your interview journey, remember that preparation is the key to success. Just like a seasoned sailor who knows their ship inside out and sails with a well-thought-out plan, you are ready to navigate the job-seeking seas confidently.

Chapter 6

Follow-Up and Feedback

Ahoy, fellow job seekers! In this chapter, I am navigating the crucial waters of follow-up and feedback, especially after your job interview. Just as a skilled captain must refine their approach based on conditions, you must adeptly steer your post-interview journey. I will guide you through the intricacies of post-interview etiquette and the art of staying connected.

6.1. Seeking Feedback to Improve Your Approach

Feedback is your compass in the job-seeking journey. We'll dive deep into why seeking feedback is vital and how to go about it.

Why Feedback Matters

Feedback is more than just words; it's a valuable tool for personal and professional growth. It acts as a guiding star in your journey, helping you navigate rough waters, identify areas for improvement, and refine your skills.

Imagine you've just had an interview that didn't lead to a job offer. Seeking feedback from your interviewers can provide invaluable insights into your performance and what you can do better next time. It's akin to a ship captain analyzing charts to understand the currents and adapt their course for smoother sailing.

Requesting Feedback

Knowing the importance of feedback is one thing; knowing how to request it effectively is another. We'll provide you with tips and strategies on how to reach out to interviewers and ask for feedback gracefully.

Consider this scenario: You've applied for a role that truly excites you, but the company decided to move forward with another candidate. Rather than feeling discouraged, you muster the courage to ask for feedback. Your email to the interviewer is courteous and thoughtful, expressing your gratitude for the opportunity and your genuine interest in improving. This proactive approach reflects your commitment to self-improvement and impresses your interviewer.

6.2. How to Handle Rejection

Rejection in the job-seeking world is like facing a storm at sea. We'll guide you on how to navigate through these challenging waters.

Resilience and Learning

It's natural to feel a range of emotions when facing rejection - disappointment, frustration, or even self-doubt. Instead of suppressing these feelings, acknowledge them. Allow yourself to experience the emotional impact of rejection fully. It's a necessary step in the healing process.

Resilience is the ability to bounce back from setbacks. Rather than dwelling on the rejection, focus on the future. Remind yourself that even the most successful individuals have faced rejection. Resilience will help you maintain the motivation to persevere.

Every rejection provides an opportunity to learn. It teaches you valuable lessons about the job market, the specific industry, and even about yourself. Over time, you become a more experienced and adaptable job seeker.

Maintaining a Positive Attitude

In the face of rejection, maintaining a positive attitude is crucial. I will offer tips on how to stay optimistic and focused on the journey ahead. Remember, every rejection is a step closer to finding the right opportunity, just as every setback at sea leads to new discoveries and adventures. Here's how to maintain that upbeat spirit:

- **Learn from Rejections:** Rejections are not failures but feedback. Use them to refine your approach and grow.
- **Visualize Success:** Keep your dream job in mind. This vision provides motivation and perspective.
- **Seek Support:** Share your journey with friends or mentors. They can offer encouragement and fresh insights.
- **Celebrate Small Wins:** Even minor victories count. They remind you that progress is being made.
- **Trust the Journey:** Understand that the right opportunity is waiting. Like a sailor trusting the stars, your path will lead you to new horizons.

In your job search voyage, remember that staying positive isn't about denying challenges but facing them with unwavering hope and resilience. Every rejection brings you closer to the right opportunity.

6.3. Ready for the Second Option

Life is full of unexpected twists and turns. We'll explore the art of being ready for the second option.

Exploring Alternatives

Sometimes, the job you didn't expect can turn out to be the perfect fit. I have mentioned below how to be open to alternative opportunities that may come your way. Just like a sailor who encounters uncharted waters, your adaptability and openness can lead you to unexpected treasures.

- **Expand Your Horizons:** Be open to different roles or industries. Your skills may translate well into new territories.
- **Network Broadly:** Talk to professionals outside your immediate field. You might discover uncharted waters worth exploring.
- **Learn Continuously:** Acquire new skills that make you more adaptable. The more versatile you are, the easier it is to pivot.
- **Follow Your Passion:** Sometimes, an unexpected opportunity aligns perfectly with your interests. Be ready to seize it.
- **Trust Your Instincts:** If a new opportunity excites you, it's worth investigating. Like a sailor charting

new courses, you might uncover unanticipated treasures.

Flexibility doesn't mean settling for less; it's about staying open to possibilities. Just as seasoned sailors adapt to shifting winds and tides, your career journey may take unexpected but fulfilling turns.

6.4. Sending Thank-You Notes and Emails

Just as a handwritten letter conveys thoughtfulness, sending thank-you notes or emails after an interview is a sign of your professionalism.

Why Send Thank-You Notes

Understand the significance of sending thank-you notes or emails and how they can set you apart from other candidates. A well-crafted thank-you note is like a message in a bottle, conveying your gratitude and your continued interest in the opportunity.

For example, sending a thank-you email after an interview is akin to a mariner sending a heartfelt note to express gratitude for safe passage. It conveys professionalism and appreciation, leaving a lasting impression on the interviewers.

Crafting the Perfect Thank-You Note

Your thank-you note should be genuine, concise, and personalized, much like a treasure map with the "X" marking your appreciation. Creating an impactful thank-you note is an art. Here are some practical tips and examples to help you craft the perfect message:

- **Be Prompt**: Send your thank-you note within 24-48 hours of the interview or receiving assistance. Timing is key.
- **Express Sincerity**: Start with a warm greeting and express your genuine gratitude for the opportunity, advice, or help.
- **Be Specific**: Mention the specific details of the interview, meeting, or assistance to show you were actively engaged.
- **Highlight Fit**: Reiterate your excitement for the position or mention how the guidance you received aligns with your goals.
- **Personalize**: Make it unique. Reference something discussed during the interview or a shared interest.
- **Address Everyone**: If you interviewed multiple people, send personalized notes to each.
- **Concise and Polished**: Keep it concise. Proofread for errors, and use a professional tone.

Example 1 - After an Interview:

Dear [Interviewer's Name],

I wanted to express my sincere gratitude for the opportunity to interview for the [Position] role at [Company]. Our conversation about [specific topic discussed] was particularly inspiring, and it reinforced my enthusiasm for the potential to contribute to your team. I look forward to the possibility of working with such a dynamic group.

Thank you once again for your time and consideration.

Best regards, [Your Name]

Example 2 - After Receiving Assistance:

Hi [Mentor's Name],

I hope this message finds you well. I wanted to extend my heartfelt thanks for the valuable insights you shared during our recent discussion about [topic]. Your advice regarding [specific advice received] was especially enlightening and has already had a positive impact on my approach.

I genuinely appreciate your guidance and am excited to put your suggestions into action. Your support means a lot to me.

Warm regards, [Your Name]

Remember, a well-crafted thank-you note can leave a strong impression and set you apart.

6.5. Stay Connected

Even after the job hunt ends, staying connected can lead to future opportunities. We'll explore the importance of building and maintaining professional relationships.

Networking Beyond the Interview

Learn how to nurture professional connections, even if you didn't secure the job.

For example, after an interview, you stay connected with the company and its employees through LinkedIn and occasional messages. This networking effort eventually leads to another opportunity in the future, showcasing the long-term benefits of maintaining connections.

As I conclude this chapter, remember that the voyage of job-seeking is a journey filled with both challenges and opportunities. The skills you've acquired, from seeking feedback and handling rejection with resilience to staying open to alternative paths, will set you on a course toward professional success. Sending those thank-you notes and nurturing connections will be your anchor in the ever-changing tides of the job market. So, as you continue your journey, keep your eyes on the horizon, for beyond the waves of rejection and uncertainty, your dream job may await.